Desert Animals

Rattlesnakes

by Emily Rose Townsend

Consulting Editor: Gail Saunders-Smith, Ph.D.

Consultant: Michael A. Mares, Ph.D.
Director, Sam Noble Oklahoma Museum
of Natural History, University of Oklahoma,
Norman, Oklahoma

Pebble Books

an imprint of Capstone Press
Mankato, Minnesota

Pebble Books are published by Capstone Press
151 Good Counsel Drive, P.O. Box 669, Mankato, Minnesota 56002
http://www.capstone-press.com

1 2 3 4 5 6 08 07 06 05 04 03

Library of Congress Cataloging-in-Publication Data
Townsend, Emily Rose.
    Rattlesnakes / by Emily Rose Townsend.
    p. cm.—(Desert animals)
    Includes bibliographical references (p. 23) and index.
    Contents: Rattlesnakes—Desert—Body—Day and night.
    ISBN 0-7368-2078-7 (hardcover)
    1. Rattlesnakes—Juvenile literature. [1. Rattlesnakes. 2. Snakes.] I. Title.
QL666.O69 T68 2004
597.96—dc21   2002154583

Summary: Simple text and photographs depict rattlesnakes that live in deserts.

Note to Parents and Teachers

The Desert Animals series supports national science standards
related to life science. This book describes and illustrates
rattlesnakes that live in deserts. The photographs support early
readers in understanding the text. The repetition of words and
phrases helps early readers learn new words. This book also
introduces early readers to subject-specific vocabulary words,
which are defined in the Glossary section. Early readers may need
assistance to read some words and to use the Table of Contents,
Glossary, Read More, Internet Sites, and Index/Word List sections
of the book.

Table of Contents

4

Rattlesnakes

Rattlesnakes are poisonous snakes. Snakes are reptiles.

Most rattlesnakes have rattles on their tails. They shake their tails when they sense danger.

8

Rattlesnakes have fangs.
Rattlesnakes bite their prey
and kill them with venom.

Rattlesnakes eat rats,
lizards, birds, and
other small animals.

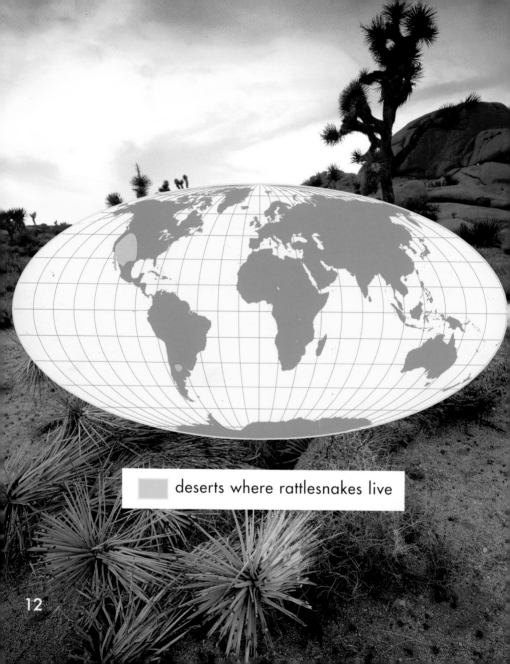

deserts where rattlesnakes live

Deserts

Many rattlesnakes live
in deserts in the United
States and Mexico.

Body

Rattlesnakes have scales.
The scales are dry.

The scales form patterns on the body of a rattlesnake.

18

Rattlesnakes shed their skin. New skin grows under the old skin.

Day and Night

Rattlesnakes stay cool under rocks during the day. They mostly hunt at night.

Glossary

desert—an area that is very dry; deserts do not get much rainfall.

fang—a long, hollow tooth

pattern—a repeated set of colors and shapes

poisonous—able to harm or kill with poison or venom

prey—an animal that is hunted by another animal for food

rattle—the end part of a rattlesnake's tail that makes a buzzing, rattling sound when it moves

reptile—a cold-blooded animal that crawls or creeps on the ground

scale—a small piece of hard skin that covers a rattlesnake's body

shed—to have something fall or drop off

venom—a poison that some snakes make; rattlesnakes have two glands in their jaw that hold venom; the venom flows through their hollow fangs into their prey.

Read More

Murray, Julie. *Rattlesnakes.* Animal Kingdom. Edina, Minn.: Abdo, 2003.

Robinson, Claire. *Snakes.* In the Wild. Chicago: Heinemann Library, 1999.

Wechsler, Doug. *Rattlesnakes.* The Really Wild Life of Snakes. New York: PowerKids Press, 2001.

Internet Sites

Do you want to find out more about rattlesnakes? Let FactHound, our fact-finding hound dog, do the research for you.

Here's how:

1) Visit *http://www.facthound.com.*

2) Type in the **Book ID** number: **0736820787**

3) Click on **FETCH IT**.

FactHound will fetch web sites picked by our editors just for you!

Index/Word List

Word Count: 96
Early-Intervention Level: 13

Editorial Credits
Mari C. Schuh, editor; Patrick D. Dentinger, book designer; Kelly Garvin,
photo researcher; Karen Risch, product planning editor

Photo Credits
Bruce Coleman Inc./Joe McDonald, 6, 14, 20; D. Lyons, 8; M.P.L. Fogden, 10;
Gary Meslars, 16
Dwight R. Kuhn, 1
Joe McDonald, cover, 4, 18
Rubberball Productions, 12